Original title:
Ties and Tears

Copyright © 2025 Creative Arts Management OÜ
All rights reserved.

Author: Oliver Bennett
ISBN HARDBACK: 978-1-80586-151-5
ISBN PAPERBACK: 978-1-80586-623-7

Unraveled and Unbound

In a world where strings get knotted,
My sock now wears a hole, it's spotted.
My cat thinks it's a playful game,
I chase it down, calling its name.

The spaghetti's swirling like a dance,
Twisting around, it won't take a chance.
The fork is laughing, the noodles flee,
As I try to trap them—oh, woe is me!

My dog looks on with a puppy grin,
As I stumble and fall, now where to begin?
A balloon slips loose, floats high and away,
Blowing a kiss, oh, what a display!

Yet in this chaos, laughter does prevail,
With silly mishaps we can regale.
Through tangled yarn and a playful fight,
We find the joy in the silly slight.

The Echo of a Breath

A hiccup jumps like a wayward frog,
Creating laughter, it jumps like a dog.
With every pause, the giggles grow,
An echo of life in a comic show.

In the kitchen, cookies burn and flop,
I dive for water—on my head, a plop!
The oven hums a mocking tune,
As smoke signals rise towards the moon.

My friend trips on a rubber boot,
His laughter echoes, oh, what a hoot!
We dance around like clumsy fools,
Breaking the rules of serious schools.

In these moments, lighthearted and bright,
We gather our joy, holding it tight.
An echo of fun in what we tackle,
Life's little blunders turn into a cackle.

Emotions Laid Bare

My socks in the dryer, they dance and spin,
Hiding from lint like it's wearing a grin.
They play hide and seek with the static delight,
Who knew laundry could spark such a fight?

In the cupboard I find a lost rubber band,
It's been waiting for years, now it's feeling grand.
It snaps with a pop, full of joy in the air,
Throwing laughs at the world, like it hasn't a care.

Stitched Together in Silence

Two mismatched mittens under the bed,
One's on a mission, the other's misled.
They sit in the dark, planning a trip,
To find the right pair, so none take a dip.

A button once lost, now holds ancient tales,
From dinner mishaps to ice cream fails.
It tells stories of feasts, of laughter and cheer,
Who knew it could make us all shed a tear?

Unraveling Moments

A shoelace that knows it can twist and twirl,
Sneaks off my shoe for its daring whirl.
But with a quick trip, it sadly resigns,
Now it's back in line, crossing the lines.

The cat takes a leap, it's a midair affair,
Chasing its tail with flair, without a care.
It wobbles and rolls, with a funny little meow,
Creating a scene that could draw quite a crowd.

Tangles of the Past

Old photographs stuck in a drawer full of dust,
Memories trapped, oh how they rust.
But when sunlight hits, they come out to play,
Wearing smiles of mischief from back in the day.

My grandma's old scarf, a rainbow of yarn,
Whispers soft secrets of love and a charm.
It wraps 'round my neck, chuckles with glee,
As if weaving tales of the world's history.

A Patchwork Heart

Stitch together bits of glee,
With frayed edges joyfully.
Colors clash, they waltz around,
In my chest, a circus found.

Needle pokes, I laugh it off,
Mismatched threads make me scoff.
Each patch tells a silly tale,
Of my heart's wild, quirky trail.

The Color of Nostalgia

Old photographs in funny hats,
Memories tucked with furry cats.
Every smile has a twist and turn,
  A history that's hard to spurn.

Faded tones, a vibrant zest,
 Naps on couches, a cozy nest.
Laughter's hue, a mix and blend,
Where the past and chuckles send.

Wounds of Affection

Bumps and bruises, oh what fun,
Kisses make the stitches run.
A playful jab, a loving shove,
Was that a bruise? Well, that's true love!

We gag on cookies, share our woes,
Each mishap comes with painted bows.
A hearty laugh, a playful shove,
These funny wounds, they fit like gloves.

Laughter Between Rips

Socks with holes, oh what a sight,
Dancing feet in pure delight.
Giggles erupt with each small tear,
Every flaw shows love and flair.

Rip my shirt? Ha! What a blast!
Fashion faux pas, unsurpassed.
In every cut, a chuckle grows,
Our spirits soar as laughter flows.

Hidden Moments

In a cupboard, snacks do hide,
Crisps and chocolate, oh what pride.
A secret feast, just me tonight,
Laughing softly, what a sight.

Bouncing cats chase their tails,
While I munch on dinner fails.
Spilled a drink, oh what a laugh,
Now I'm part of the aftermath.

The Quiet Aftermath

A prank went off, it was quite grand,
Silly string flew, oh wasn't planned.
Friends are laughing, floor covered in goo,
What a sight, we're stuck like glue.

We wrangle the mess, in laughter we cheer,
Shoving each other, too much cheer.
With every splatter, joy is found,
In chaos, we dance, spinning around.

Bridges of Emotion

Belly laughs spark, then burst in spree,
Silly faces shared by you and me.
A wink, a nudge, we're side by side,
Building bridges with fun as our guide.

Though sometimes we stumble, trip, or fall,
We rise again, just to have a ball.
With giggles and jests, our hearts will soar,
Creating moments, who could ask for more?

A Collection of What Was

In boxes lie memories, wrapped up tight,
Mismatched socks and a kid's delight.
Photos of faces making a fuss,
When life was simply endless plus.

Shenanigans captured in playful frames,
Each smile a puzzle, none are the same.
As we flick through, oh what a ride,
In nostalgia's grip, laughter won't hide.

Love's Fragility

In the game of hearts, we laugh and play,
But drop the ball and hear it sway.
A spaghetti strand that's falling apart,
We giggle and sigh; it's just the start.

Like a rubber band stretched far too thin,
We tug at the edges; oh, where to begin?
A bouquet of daisies, wilting might be,
But oh, what a circus of comedy!

A Drift of Seconds

Time's a prankster, it tickles our feet,
With seconds that dance, and hours that cheat.
We whizz past each other, a blur in the fray,
Holding our laughter like ice cream in May.

Socks in a dryer, they tumble and spin,
Each mismatched moment, where one is a twin.
Like trying to catch smoke with a grin,
We wave as it drifts, let the nonsense begin!

The Distance Between Us

Your laugh is a balloon, so high in the sky,
I stretch for the string, but it flutters by.
It tickles the clouds and does such a dance,
While I'm stuck on the ground, wishing for a chance.

Like a pizza slice dropping at dinner with flair,
It slips from my fingers; oh, what a scare!
We chuckle at distance, it stretches the fun,
A game of tag where we're always outdone!

Knotted Memories

In the attic of time, where old jokes reside,
We sift through the laughter that's tangled inside.
A shoelace of mishaps, twisted but bright,
Each memory dances, a comedic sight.

Like a cat in a tree with a flip and a flop,
The moments we share, we can't quite stop.
In the scrapbook of goofs, we glue down the cheer,
With sparkles of giggles, let's give them a cheer!

Unspoken Threads

In a room full of socks, some disappear,
Like my sanity when the cat comes near.
With every laundry, chaos appears,
Yet I laugh at the mess, my face in cheer.

In the fridge, an old pizza stands tall,
Its life has been longer than most of us all.
We share our secrets, as I grab a slice,
What can I say? It's not so precise.

My friend wears mismatched shoes in a rush,
I giggle and tease him, 'You're quite the plush!'
He shrugs with a grin, and so we agree,
That style is subjective, even with glee.

In the end, we all dance on thin air,
With laughter and quirks, life's quite the affair.
Though some things may unravel, don't take it to heart,
Just find joy in the mess, that's the finest art.

Ribbons and Ruins

There's a spool of ribbon that's rolled away,
Like my brain in Mondays, gone astray.
I search high and low, uncovering dust,
Turns out it was hiding in the back of my bust.

A cupcake fell down from the counter so high,
With frosting splattered, oh me, oh my!
Where's the storm that made it topple and twist?
Must've been sweet gravity, too good to resist.

My dog wears a bow, thinks he's quite the chap,
With a meadow of flowers nestled on his lap.
And when he prances, we all stand amazed,
At the fashion statements that leave us dazed.

Chaos and charm in mismatched delight,
Life's a big puzzle that twists day and night.
So let's raise a toast to the mismatched and bright,
And laugh through the ruins till morning light.

Fragments of Longing

In the fridge, two leftovers have a debate,
One's a soggy noodle, the other, a plate.
They ponder their purpose as I stroll by,
And I pause to chuckle, unsure who'll comply.

A paperplane launched from a child's fair hand,
Is lost to the wind, though it tried to withstand.
It flutters and flops like a fish out of water,
While the kid just giggles, filled with pure laughter.

Love notes still cling to the fridge with tape,
All faded and wrinkled, each lovingly shaped.
Though words now seem silly, they spark a bright smile,
As I read 'fore dinner, such wit was worthwhile!

And in all these moments, the stumbles and fails,
We find that our joys are like spontaneous trails.
So let's gather our whims, with quirks that we bring,
And dance like balloons on a cold spring fling.

The Weight of Silver Linings

I wore my best hat on a windy day,
It flew off like a bird that's lost its way.
Chasing that hat was a sight to behold,
As I dodged the neighbors, feeling quite bold.

With donuts in hand, I tried to impress,
But icing, much like me, is quite prone to stress.
I slipped on a sprinkle, it acted like glue,
And landed in laughter, oh what a view!

My car's taken on a life of its own,
With a music playlist that's loudly overgrown.
A dance in the front seat, I'm feeling sublime,
Guess who's offbeat? That would be my rhyme.

As we twirl with our mishaps, in joyous delight,
The weight of our worries just takes flight,
So let's celebrate life with all its odd clings,
Finding humor and peace in the wild and the swings.

Fleeting Echoes

In the hall where laughter bounces,
A whoopee cushion found its place,
A hidden trap for solemn pounces,
Each squeak a grin, a joyful race.

A cat who thinks it's got the moves,
Slides right off the fancy chair,
It swats the air, the rhythm grooves,
While I just try to catch my air.

Jokes that fall, but smiles still rise,
Like pancakes flipping in the sun,
With every flop, a new surprise,
And laughter plays, we have our fun.

In memory's quilt, the stitches fray,
And yet those gaps are filled with cheer,
A dance to songs that fade away,
But echoes linger, crystal clear.

Woven Dreams

The knitting club now spins a tale,
Of sweaters made for ice cream scoops,
They laugh so hard, they start to wail,
As yarn becomes a mode for loops.

The cat, it thinks it's part of art,
In every ball, a tangled twist,
While we just watch, and do our part,
In laughter's game, we can't resist.

A hiccup mixed with tricks and pranks,
As muffins fly like shooting stars,
The table shakes with all our thanks,
For crumbs and giggles, none from bars.

While dreams we stitch may change their seams,
Each thread a smile, a little jest,
In woven tales of silly dreams,
We find the joy that feels the best.

Rippled Reflections

The mirror shows a funny face,
With popcorn stuck to every cheek,
A dance-off in a wobbly space,
Where moves are awkward, yet unique.

Each giggle causes mighty waves,
A splash of joy, we can't be tamed,
The silly things we do and crave,
Leave us all smiling, never shamed.

A rubber duck becomes a star,
Bobbling in a tub of cheer,
We sing off-key, we won't go far,
Yet every look's a happy smear.

In puddles, laughter starts to blend,
And ripples carry all our fun,
For in this world, with joy to spend,
Our mirrored selves are never done.

Fractured Promises

I swore I'd bake the best souffle,
Yet found a cake that looked like goo,
With frosting mishaps on display,
A treat that made us all go 'Whooo!'

A promise made to dance so slick,
Yet tripped upon an unseen shoe,
We laughed so hard, it made us thick,
In joy we found the silly crew.

A slip on ice, a spritz of cheer,
With snowflakes stuck upon my nose,
I fumble through; it's crystal clear,
These fractured bits form silly prose.

For every blunder, giggles rise,
As joy is stitched with goofy threads,
In joyful chaos, laughter flies,
And hugs are shared where fun embeds.

Unspoken Goodbyes

The cat wore a suit, it looked quite bizarre,
We waved at it proudly, from here, it flew far.
With fish in its pocket, it danced on the stage,
A farewell so silly, we laughed through the page.

The doorbell rang loudly, a ghost said goodbye,
It tripped on a rug, oh my, how it did fly!
With a wink and a nod, as it vanished from view,
We chuckled at shadows, bidding adieu.

Whispers of the Heart

The parrot sang secrets, all lies dressed in cheer,
It squawked about love, yet held back its beer.
With one eye on dinner, and the other on fate,
We giggled as it crooned, oh isn't that great?

A wink from the toaster, it popped out a puff,
Burnt edges of dreams, it was never enough.
We toasted to tailwinds, with jelly on bread,
And lived for the moments, too funny to dread.

Fragments of Faith

A shoe on the roof claimed a brilliant new start,
It swayed in the breeze, with a mind and a heart.
With echoes of laughter, it swore it would stay,
Yet clouds came to chuckle, and carried it away.

The moon wore a smile, as stars told a joke,
In the carnival of night, the shadows awoke.
With flickers of nonsense, they danced in delight,
In fragments of nonsense, we laughed through the night.

Mending the Invisible

A sock lost its partner, they fought like a pair,
In a game of thrones, both floating in air.
It twirled on the floor, a warrior with dreams,
While we found entertainment in fabric it seems.

The chair tried to whisper, "Let's patch up our woes,"
But it squeaked its confession, and right then it froze.
With laughter abundant, we rallied the crew,
To mend the invisible, with giggles anew.

The Fragile Thread

In the laundry room, socks roam free,
Hoping to find a mate, just like me.
Was it the washer that caused this rift?
Or just a game of sock-thief drift?

Lost my left shoe on a wild day,
Now it's solo dance with no ballet.
My laces look more like a sculptor's art,
Each knot a whisper of a broken heart.

Heartstrings Unraveled

I tried to juggle, but one fell down,
Now I'm the clown wearing a frown.
A juggling act of love, what a sight!
When romance crashes, it's pure delight.

Can someone tell me where my marbles went?
'Cause love's a game that's often bent.
Each date a laugh, then a strange goodbye,
With mismatched socks and a lopsided tie.

Echoes of Longing

Echoes bounce when the fridge door creaks,
Memories stored in the leftover leaks.
Cupcake crumbs dance on the tablecloth,
A sugar high that soon fades, oh what a swath!

With every bite, a giggle erupts,
Like trying to fix a watch that interrupts.
The joy of cooking leads to silly spills,
Mixing spices just gives me more thrills.

Tattered Bonds

Friendship bracelets made of yarn,
Until a cat thought it was a charm.
Chasing tails as the colors fly,
Guess my fashion's not that spry!

Slippers that squeak, and hats that clash,
My wardrobe's a real comedic bash.
Stitching together moments so bright,
Even in chaos, we unite with delight.

Embracing the Unraveling

Once we laughed over lost socks,
Chasing feel-good vibes in our paradox.
With every twist, our bond's a game,
Not quite tearing, but never the same.

We dance through all our tangled lines,
A messy waltz of silly designs.
When life pulls tight, we let it roll,
Witty quips are how we console.

In chaos, humor makes us smile,
With every slip, we hear the style.
Like kittens pouncing on a ball,
We're a circus, together we fall.

So here's to chaos, don't you fret,
It's in the jest that we're truly set.
With laughter as our gentle guide,
We embrace the quirks we can't abide.

Ghosts of Connection

In the attic of my mind they roam,
Nostalgic whispers feel like home.
They poke and prod, till I can't breathe,
A chuckle here, a sigh, then leave.

Past friendships drift like phantom ships,
On waves of laughter, through muted lips.
Eerie echoes in a haunting dance,
In every glance, a fleeting chance.

We raise our glasses to the missed,
To moments gone that still persist.
These spirits tease, with glimmers bright,
In a spectral glow, they ignite delight.

So here's to shadows made of cheer,
A ghostly laugh that lingers near.
For though they fade, their charms remain,
A joyful haunt that's never mundane.

Traces of Joy

In the garden where giggles bloom,
Sprinkled lights push away the gloom.
With every petal, a story unfolds,
Of playful pranks and laughter bold.

We trip on roots and dance on air,
Bumbling our way through carefree flair.
Each step a memory, lightly kept,
In the scrapbook of where we leapt.

Sprouts of joy amidst the mess,
Life's a riddle wrapped in finesse.
Caught in the whirlwind, we find our rhyme,
With every blunder, a laugh -- sublime.

So let's toast to the whimsical play,
With each wrong turn, we find our way.
For in the quirks and silly plights,
The traces of joy light up our nights.

Memories Like Threads

In grandma's quilt, the patches fight,
Each color's tale spun with delight.
Stories woven, a ruffled hall,
Laughter stitch by stitch through it all.

We gather 'round, with needles in hand,
Knots of chaos all carefully planned.
A button here, a yarn to braid,
Through thick and thin, we've always stayed.

On rainy days, we spin the yarn,
Tall tales of hope that never sharn.
We mend the gaps with silly plays,
Reminding us to cherish our days.

So here's to fabric, old and new,
Stitched by snafus, bright sunshine too.
The thread of laughter never frays,
In every loop, our heartstrings play.

A tapestry of Longing

A sock went missing, oh what a plight,
Its partner awaits, day and night.
In the laundry jungle, it made a run,
Perhaps it's off dancing, having some fun.

The lonely shoe, it starts to whine,
Wishing for a mate, some fancy design.
They say opposites attract, what a jest!
But in this closet, they fail the test.

Threads of Fate

In a world where kittens claim the floor,
And hats fly off each time you roar.
Fate pulls a thread, and what a twist,
You find your clothes in a tangled mist.

Socks whisper secrets in the dryer's spin,
While the coats argue, who let the cat in?
Fate's stitching laughter into the seams,
As lost underwear pursues its dreams.

Jagged Memories

A sandwich fell, oh what a sight,
The mustard splatted, gave quite a fright.
Forks and knives, they gather 'round,
To reminisce when dishes were crowned.

Once I dropped a cake, a glorious fall,
It rolled away like it had a ball.
I still hear laughter from an old friend's face,
As we chased that dessert all over the place.

Heartstrings in the Wind

A kite once soared, caught in a tree,
Its colors bright, a sight to see.
But branches snickered, gave it a hug,
As it dangled there, feeling quite smug.

The breeze carried giggles, up to the sky,
As squirrels plotted, wondering why.
Strings danced merrily, a whimsical chase,
In the wind's embrace, they found their place.

Bonds Unraveled

Once I tried to knit a sock,
But ended up with quite a shock.
Two left feet sat on my floor,
Now I have one and want no more.

My friend said, "Let's shoot some darts,"
I aimed and hit my own two hearts.
He laughed so hard he lost his breath,
A friendship sealed in near death.

We pledged to share our deepest woes,
Instead, we laughed at silly shows.
Our secrets turned to comic strips,
With punchlines curled on friendship's lips.

When bonds get quirky, heads are spun,
We dance like fools while having fun.
In every mix-up, life's a blast,
These moments shine, forever cast.

Frayed Connections

A phone call placed, but who's to say,
My cat meowed and stole the day.
I spilled my beans, she drank my tea,
And now we're bound, her and me.

We tried to fix a bike's old chain,
But ended up in deep disdain.
I spun the wheel, she lost her shoe,
Who knew repair could be so blue?

With jumbled words and laughter loud,
We tripped through life, a bumbling crowd.
Each slip was met with joyous cheer,
In every mess, we held our near.

Connections frayed, yet strong they're found,
In tangled jokes, our joys abound.
Though life may stretch and sometimes tear,
We weave our stories with silly flair.

Shadows of Yesterday

We played charades and bumped our heads,
A shadow dance, with mischief spread.
I said, "I'm strong!" while tripping back,
My pride was bruised, my ego cracked.

Oh, the things we thought we knew,
Like how to cook, then burned the stew.
The laughter echoed through the night,
As memories faded in the light.

We wore our hearts right on our sleeves,
Yet silence fell a lot, like leaves.
With nods and winks, we shared our food,
The joke was clear, and so was the mood.

The past is funny, twisty too,
With shadows that we dance on through.
Though time may fade, this truth's so bright,
Our silly moments are pure delight.

Echoes of Heartstrings

A serenade gone dreadfully wrong,
My guitar shrieked a silly song.
We laughed so hard, I lost my pick,
Thought music easy—oh, what a trick!

In the games we played, we lost our way,
Spilled soda bright on a summer's day.
Our laughter echoed, a joyful ring,
With every mishap, our hearts would sing.

We shared our dreams of golden skies,
But ended up with goofy pies.
Life threw us curves, yet we held tight,
In chaos found our purest light.

The echoes dance, a rippling thrill,
In every giggle, we've found our fill.
Through silly moments, our bonds grow strong,
Together we laugh, forever belong.

Weaving Fragments

In a quilt of laughter, all the bits
Stitched together, gaps and knits.
Snag one corner, and watch it swirl,
A jumble of patterns, a colorful whirl.

A patch of whimsy, a smudge of glee,
Here's a patch that annoys me.
A bobble of giggles, a fray or two,
  Sewing sanity back in, who knew?

Each peekaboo square holds a tale untold,
Some fuzzy, some bright, all are bold.
When life unravels, we mend with cheer,
Grab the old fabric, bring it near.

So let's whip up a fabric made of smiles,
A collage of flops that stretch for miles.
In this crazy quilt, our hearts will mend,
  With every stitch, let the laughter blend.

A Stitch in Time

One stitch away from losing my mind,
Spools of laughter, you often find.
Threading jokes in every seam,
A fashion trend, or so it seems.

Came a gap wider than my grin,
What's left to dangle, let the fun begin!
A needle later, and look who's back,
In a wardrobe full of humorous flack.

Patches of whimsy on every shirt,
Wear them proudly, with a little dirt.
Laugh lines fray, but it's not a crime,
Just a snazzy remnant, a stitch in time.

So swing your fabric, salsa your thread,
Embrace the chaos, dance instead.
With every twist and every loop,
We find the fun in this crazy group.

Melodies of Departure

Chords of laughter in an empty room,
Where socks have vanished, meet their doom.
Every note a tear, so wild and free,
What a symphony of missing spree!

With flailing arms, we wave goodbye,
To coffee mugs and the donut pie.
A serenade of silly mischief,
In this jest, we find our relief.

Each whimsical tune, a silly march,
Back and forth like a hasty arch.
Musical chairs but with some flair,
One wrong move, land in a chair!

As we pack our bags, let laughter reign,
In departures that sprout joy, not pain.
For memories linger, in melody's grace,
Where funny prevails, we find our place.

The Lament of Lost Embrace

A hug went missing, what a bizarre flight,
Tangled limbs and laughter ignite.
Oh, Marco Polo in a cuddle maze,
Where'd you go? In this funny haze!

Fumbled with pillows, flopped on the floor,
Searching high, but I need more.
With every turn, giggles ensue,
As I lose my grip on this moment with you.

Rolling in laughter, an upside-down spin,
Lost hugs lead to more grins within.
Every twirl, a twist of delight,
Who needs balance when you've got flight?

So here's to the hugs that dart and dash,
The funny moments that are bound to clash.
Embrace the chaos, let laughter fly,
In the dance of the lost, we'll give it a try.

Faded Connections

In the attic sit old shoes,
Sock puppets singing the blues.
One's tangled, the other's frayed,
Yet together they often played.

They dance on strings of silly plight,
And giggle through the fall of night.
Old friends with a pinch of dust,
Laughing like they surely must.

With every wink, nostalgia calls,
As faces fade on dusty walls.
A friend left behind, who would care?
Fun times still float in the air.

A burst, a pop, oh what a laugh!
With friends like these, who needs a path?
Through knots and loops, they shimmy and sway,
In a friendship, come what may.

The Color of Sorrow

A rainbow spills from a cloudy sky,
But rainstains fade as puddles dry.
With every drip, a chuckle flows,
As laughter hides in muddy rows.

A painter dabs a brush on grey,
With colors bright that splash and play.
Slips of humor, a dog on a bike,
Patchworks of hope that giggle and hike.

When laughter wears a funny mask,
That's when joy becomes the task.
A teardrop perched on a clown's nose,
Turns to chuckles where silliness grows.

So splash those colors, let them bright,
In a hue that brings delight.
Through the grins, the laughs, the glow,
Life's a canvas, let it flow.

Dreams Unspooled

A dream unspooled like tangled yarn,
Spinning tales that cause no harm.
Caught in giggles, shadows chase,
While silly grins light up the space.

With every twist, a whimsy found,
As pillows fight and roll around.
The night rumbles with playful glee,
In a world of dreams, all things are free.

Each spooling twist a chuckle makes,
A jester's hat, a dance that shakes.
Through goofy hops and silly sings,
Joy unravels in little flings.

So gather 'round with laughter sound,
In dreams where whimsy is unbound.
Through that spool of dreams we jest,
Life's a prank, and we're the best.

The Echoes of Binding

Two strings that twirl with lots of flair,
Each tug a giggle, without a care.
In this dance, we go offbeat,
Yet find the rhythm in our feet.

The echoes bounce with every pull,
As laughter fills the air so full.
Tight-knit jokes tie up the night,
With smiles wrapped up, oh what a sight!

When bonds are forged with silly glee,
A raucous crew of irony.
From every stitch, a tale is spun,
This party of laughter has just begun.

So cling tight, friends, and take your chance,
In the echoes, we twist and dance.
With joy that binds and pulls us near,
In this glass of laughter, let's cheer!

Threads of a Story

In a land where laughter sews,
A button lost, the fabric grows.
Oh, the quilt of silly fights,
Wrapped in warmth on chilly nights.

Pants that shrank when washed too hot,
Friends who tease, but tie the knot.
A thread that zips, a fabric laugh,
The seamstress of a friendship path.

Hats that flew on windy days,
Socks that danced in funny ways.
Each stitch brings a tale so dear,
Weaving joy from every tear.

So let's spin the yarn with cheer,
In every twist, a tale we hear.
With every knot, a story made,
In this silly fabric parade.

Erosion of Affection

Two hearts once bold now fall apart,
Lost in the ocean of a fart.
Sands of laughter, grains of glee,
Erode the love like waves at sea.

Cuddles turned to laughs and cries,
When pizza baked and burnt the fries.
Each moment slips through fingers quick,
Like slipping on a candy slick.

Witty jabs that were once cute,
Now just sound like cheesy lute.
But through the storm, we'll surely float,
On life's grand, absurd little boat.

So here's to laughs and silly fights,
To coping with our funny plights.
Though affection shifts and sways,
We'll find humor in our days.

Chains of the Past

A link of laughter by my side,
In the closet where ghosts reside.
Old jokes echo against the wall,
Each chuckle brings our memories tall.

From mismatched socks to laughter wild,
The mishaps of a careless child.
Chains we forged through fumbles and slips,
With every flip, a comic script.

Oh, how the past can play its tricks,
Like rubber bands that flick and stick.
Yet in this rust, there's joy to find,
A quirky tale that's intertwined.

So let's embrace the links we've spun,
Turning old battles into fun.
For every chain that holds us tight,
Is a laugh waiting to take flight.

Shifting Sands of Emotion

In a desert where giggles bloom,
We dance like grains that shift and zoom.
The dunes of dreams rise and then drop,
While we trip over, hop after hop.

A wave of feelings, soft like silk,
But oh, the blunders make us milk.
Sandcastles that collapse in glee,
Bring laughter like waves from the sea.

With every twist of fate's own hand,
We surf the highs on this fine sand.
Our laughter echoes, a playful cheer,
As we navigate our way from here.

So let's ride the tide, don't hesitate,
In the shifting sands, we'll celebrate.
For every wobble, stumble, cheer,
Is just a joy that's oh-so-near.

The Silence of Parting

One shoe was left in the dance hall,
The other got lost, oh so small.
A sock found a home in a poodle's fluff,
Their separation was really quite tough.

The cake was a hit, but the fork had fled,
A silent goodbye, with crumbs instead.
The napkin waved as it took to the floor,
No more mess, or so it swore.

A joke was made 'bout forgetting your phone,
Yet the charger was left all alone.
In the chaos of laughter, someone forgot,
It seems not all was binding, or caught.

With a wink and a grin, we waved it away,
The party had left but we still had our play.
Just a moment of fun, a glimpse of the past,
And the threads we held, slipped away so fast.

Forgotten Fabric

A coat on the rack waves goodbye to the wall,
While the pants cry, 'Hey, I've had a great fall!'
The shirt's on a hanger, dreaming of dates,
But where are the shoes? Oh, they're sharing some plates!

The sweater thinks 'cozy' while stuck in the wash,
The belt's off playing, and giving a toss.
Amidst all the fun, a button did break,
Yet still, in good humor, no one gets a ache.

The colors are chasing the shadows away,
The fabric is giggling, come join in the play!
With a tumble in laughter, they roll on the floor,
In the world of the forgotten, there's friendship galore.

Who knew a closet could harbor such cheer?
With socks on escapades, our worries they clear.
Oh what a tale in a wardrobe so bright,
Where what's lost comes together, like day into night.

Lost in the Weave

The yarn took a spin, doing pirouettes,
While knitting needles laughed, making bets.
A scarf got dizzy in a round of 'what's next?',
Getting tangled in giggles, oh what a hex!

The fiber took off, like a bird on the run,
While a thread nearby said, 'This isn't much fun!'
Amidst all the stitches, one loop caught a breeze,
And off it did float, with the utmost of ease.

A bobbin jumped in, claiming a dance,
But tripped on a stitch, lost all of its chance.
The loom sat and chuckled, weaving tales of old,
Where laughter unraveled, and joy was retold.

In the mesh of the craft, no fiber felt sad,
For the jests they shared made connection not bad.
In the thread and the fluff, we found common ground,
Where losing it all only made us more sound.

Chords of Remorse

A trumpet once sang, but forgot all its notes,
While the tuba just chuckled and jiggled its odes.
A violin plucked at the heartstrings with flair,
But the harp sighed and whispered, 'I'm stuck in mid-air!'

The drum rolled its eyes, feeling somewhat ignored,
As the flutes played a prank, giving silence awards.
A choir of chuckles erupted from deep,
Leaving behind a melody that wanted to leap.

A guitar strummed low, with a strum and a sigh,
Saying, 'Where's my buddy? He waved me goodbye.'
While the stand-up bass made a joke from the bass,
Turning sorrow to laughter, with musical grace.

In the key of the mood, where regret takes a bow,
The harmony blooms and unites us somehow.
For every missed note, there's a punchline to chase,
In this orchestra of life, there's no room for disgrace.

The Fabric of Farewell

In a quilt of chuckles, we wave goodbye,
Stitching memories where laughter can fly.
Our fabric frays but with colors so bright,
Each thread a giggle, a warm, fuzzy light.

With bumpy seams that are quite the sight,
We'll patch up the gaffes, oh what a delight!
Snagged on a sock, a tale we will spin,
To mend all the moments that made us all grin.

Broken Links

A chain of mishaps, oh what a show,
Each link is a laugh, it's wild, don't you know?
With jumbled connections and goofy designs,
We trip on our laughter, lost in the lines.

A loop made of giggles, a twist that we seek,
In tangled up moments, it's humor we leak.
So raise up your glasses to blunders in sync,
A toast to our bonds that make us all clink!

Gentle Fractures

A crack in the laughter, a giggle escapes,
In small little gaps, we uncover our shapes.
With broadening smiles and a wink of the eye,
We dance through the chaos, oh me, oh my!

Each crack tells a story, each split has its beat,
In happy disasters, our joy's bittersweet.
With every odd moment, our spirits do soar,
In the tapestry of fun, we find evermore.

Love's Paradox

In a game of warm hugs that often get lost,
We juggle our hearts, but at what little cost?
With shrugs that embrace all our quirks and our flaws,
We laugh at the mess and just give it applause.

Through bumbles and fumbles, we dance through the night,
In love's funny puzzles, it's sheer delight.
So come share a chuckle, let's relish the scene,
In the jumble of life, we're all just routine.

Remnants of Affection

A sock stuck in the dryer spin,
My heart, it feels the pull within.
You stole my fries, I rolled my eyes,
Yet laughter echoes, no goodbyes.

Remember when we danced at noon?
Your feet stepped on my pet raccoon.
We giggled loud, the neighbors stared,
In all our chaos, love was shared.

We opened gifts wrapped tight with care,
Found a hairball in the air.
Old teddy bears and half-baked dreams,
We stitched our joys with silly schemes.

In life's great mess, we often trip,
Yet still we hold with a firm grip.
Through all the quirks and silly fights,
We build our world with silly lights.

Stitches of Remembering

A band-aid on a laughing heart,
Our laughter's art, a messy part.
Each memory has a knot or two,
Yet somehow, it feels good and true.

In photo booths with goofy props,
You made me snort, the giggles swap.
With every slip and blunder, bliss,
We patched our days with moments missed.

Your wardrobe fails, oh what a sight,
A tie worn crooked, pants too tight.
We tumble through our silly days,
Stitching love in funny ways.

With laughter's thread, we weave our tale,
Through ups and downs, we shall prevail.
As time rolls by, stay close, my friend,
Our funny bond shall never end.

The Space Between Us

A couch too small for two to fit,
Yet here we are, a cozy bit.
With snacks divided, crumbs abound,
In this cramped chaos, joy is found.

You steal the blanket, what a trick,
While I pretend it's all for kicks.
Our talks of life go on for days,
In this small space, love plays its ways.

No personal space when phones collide,
Yet somehow, that's where love resides.
We bump and laugh, it's quite a scene,
A silly dance in the in-between.

So here we stay, in this tight nook,
With playful jabs and laughter's hook.
Though far apart, we feel it here,
In every giggle, you're always near.

Moments Left Behind

A shoe beneath the sofa's clasp,
A moment lost in a silly gasp.
Forgotten naps and ice cream spills,
Our youth, it dances, gives us thrills.

The time we thought to paint the walls,
But splashed more paint than in the halls.
With splatters bright and faces blank,
You laughed so hard, we barely drank.

Pet goldfish gone but hearts remain,
Its bowl was quite the grand old bane.
Yet through the giggles, tears will dry,
In midst of folly, we still fly.

Every moment like a sticker,
Some fade fast, while others flicker.
So hold those laughs, don't let them go,
In each sweet moment, love will grow.

A Frayed Silence

In a room where whispers roam,
A cat sneezed and broke the dome.
The dog just stared, in sheer surprise,
While curtains fluttered like alive flies.

Chairs creaked like old jokes retold,
As laughter slipped through cracks so bold.
The clock tick-tocked with a snicker,
Time seemed to giggle, a little quicker.

Scattered socks made a mess of style,
Each pair out to walk their own mile.
A rogue shoe danced with cheeky flair,
While we just chuckled at the pair's despair.

Amidst this chaos, fun outlines,
Glimmers of joy in silly signs.
In this frayed silence, we found our cheer,
With laughter echoing far and near.

Through the Gaps

In a garden where weeds decide,
A gnome giggles with nowhere to hide.
Flowers debate with ants on the floor,
While squirrels plot their next little score.

A breeze tickles petals, they dance away,
As shadows stretch, play hide and sway.
Bumblebees argue who's the best flier,
Each buzzing boast sounds like a choir.

Through the gaps in laughter and cheer,
We find joy hidden, a sight so dear.
Jokes sprout like wildflowers in bloom,
Turning the dull into a cartoon.

Life's little moments burst through the seams,
Unraveled giggles, like whimsical dreams.
In this chaos, we cheer and clap,
Finding joy in each silly mishap.

Love's Anemone

In a world where hearts overreact,
A fish wore glasses — a curious act.
It squinted at bubbles floating near,
As laughter bubbled up with cheer.

Starlings flocked in comedic style,
Chasing their tails in a feathery file.
Each chirp fluffed like a joke on a page,
In the theatre of nature, oh, the stage!

A clumsy dancer, the moon took a slip,
Landing in waves with a splash and a flip.
The tides all chuckled, waves clapped their hands,
Making funny fish fry in funny bands.

In this bloom where surprises swam,
Laughter adorned with a cheeky jam.
And in this moment, we'll cheer anew,
For love's anemone shows us what's true.

The Weight of Echoes

In a hall where echoes like to play,
Laughter ricochets in a quirky ballet.
A whisper tip-toes, trying to sneak,
But bumps into giggles, it's feeling meek.

Chasing shadows like playful pups,
The echoes leap, do little jumps.
Every soft sound carries a joke,
Turning the mundane into a yoke.

A clatter of spoons and forks join the fray,
As the kitchen cringes in a clumsy display.
Plates wobble, a rebellion on the shelf,
Dancing to rhythms of laughter itself.

In this merry cacophony we find,
The weight of echoes does unwind.
In each little chuckle and whimsical shout,
We gather our joy, that's what it's about.

Threads of Memory

In the closet, my old jeans laugh,
They stretched so much, now they're a gaffe.
Each thread is a tale, a whimsical ride,
Yet here I am, with a belly to hide.

Socks gone rogue, mismatched in pairs,
One's on an adventure, the other's in flares.
I search for the mate, but they seem to flee,
Maybe they're off living more wild and free!

Grandma's knitting, a colorful yarn,
She said it was love, but it just caused alarm.
A sweater so big, it's a portable tent,
It's cozy and warm, now I'm stuck, what a dent!

Every sweater, a hug, or so I believed,
But in every reunion, more threads get retrieved.
So I'll knit out a smile, let the humor unfold,
In the tapestry of life, our memories are bold.

Shadows of Attachment

My goldfish swims round, a loop-de-loop,
But each little splash is a dramatic scoop.
He seems to attach—but just to the glass,
Oh, the joys of real love, they rarely last!

A pet rock's my friend, no fuss, no fight,
We hang on the shelf, watch day turn to night.
But it won't share secrets like fish in a bowl,
Yet rocking a rock is a quirky ol' goal!

A cat with attitude, proud on the chair,
By the way that she purrs, you would think she cares.
But when food time rolls, it's a loud siren song,
Her love is assured, but fleeting—oh, wrong!

A dance in the kitchen, with broom as my guide,
We spin with the shadows; they glide side by side.
Is it just me, or did the cat take a bow?
In this comedic chaos, where's the fun? Can I wow?

The Art of Letting Go

I planned a grand party for one, it was great,
But my cake's so big, it nailed the front gate.
I invited my friends, but they brought their snacks,
Now my dreams of dessert are piled up in packs!

Balloons in the air, they float high and proud,
But some tried to dance, and popped, way too loud.
"Don't take life so serious!" my buddy would say,
But I just spilled punch on the cat—oh, what a play!

I found a lost sock, it was out of control,
But it laughed and I chuckled, oh, what a role!
It danced through the room like it had a grand plan,
And taught me the art of being a fan.

So here's to the dreams that slip through our hands,
To the mess of our parties, and life's crazy strands.
Letting go can be funny, a comedic show,
I'll cherish the laughter, and just let it flow!

Shattered Promises

I promised to diet, but pizza's so sly,
It whispers my name, and I can't help but cry.
Like a lovesick fool, I dive into cheese,
Forget the salad—let's party with ease!

I said I'd wake early, catch sun on the rise,
But snooze is my ally, a master in lies.
The morning light beams with a puny glance,
Oh well, there's always tomorrow to dance!

I vowed to stop shopping—now look at my floor,
Clothes piled like mountains, I can't close the door.
Each piece tells a tale, of fashion gone wrong,
But they make me feel good, like a kicky, wild song!

So here's to the promises, shattered and bright,
To the funny mischief that fills up the night.
Life is too short, let's giggle and sway,
With laughs in our pockets, we'll dance through the fray!

The Weight of Remnants

In the closet, old hats stack,
Faded memories on the rack.
Trousers that fit but only in dreams,
Lurking there, plotting their schemes.

A shoe with a story, a tale so grand,
But it hops like a frog on mismatched land.
Pants that once boogied, now make a fuss,
Chasing the cat like it's a bus!

Old letters scribbled, your doodles unkind,
Each scribble whispers, "I meant to unwind."
Yet there they lay in pages so bold,
Ruining my stories, if truth be told!

So I sift through the remnants, the giggles we had,
A treasure of quirks, it's making me glad.
For as we grow wrinkled, and fashions may fade,
Laughter still sticks like the glue we made.

Silent Goodbyes

Socks that have vanished, a sneaky retreat,
One's cozy in slippers, the other's discreet.
The other, perhaps in a Bermuda sand,
Whispers of travels, oh, wasn't it grand?

Mismatched companions, they giggle and knoop,
Claiming lost lands in the laundry loop.
Their secret rendezvous, a sock puppet show,
While I'm left guessing, 'Where did you go?'

The fridge hums softly a bass in the night,
As leftovers plot an escape in their flight.
One spice jar's sighing, the herbs all conspire,
To turn my bland dinner into culinary fire.

So toast to the farewells that go without fuss,
In kitchens and closets, there's always a plus.
For every good bye brings a story anew,
Crammed in the corners, waiting for you.

In the Company of Ghosts

Boo! Said the chairs when I sat down quick,
Pillows all chuckled, a soft little trick.
Blankets rolled over, they giggled in folds,
Imaginary friends in their magical molds.

A teacup just winked, it was brimming with cheek,
"Come sip with me, darling, don't you feel freak?"
Perhaps there's a spirit stuck in my mug,
Whispering secrets, or giving a shrug.

Dust bunnies dance on the floor in delight,
As I scrape the cobwebs, their wonder ignites.
"Hey, don't disturb us, we're grooving so fine!
We were here long before, now we call it divine!"

So I'll make my peace with the shadows and laughs,
And share my old couch with their silly craft.
In the company of phantoms, I finally see,
This quirky abode is a party for me!

Hues of Longing

The red paint on walls whispers stories of glee,
While green chairs swish in a breezy decree.
The blue vase remembers the clink of a toast,
In colors of laughter, it's you that I boast.

Yellow curtains flutter, their dance makes me smile,
Recalling the moments we lingered a while.
Their playful embrace, a waltz in the air,
Together we tangled, our hearts laid bare.

Orange flames crackle, with warmth in their glow,
Recalling deep secrets they promise to show.
The colors unite like a jubilant band,
Painting a canvas of friendship so grand.

So let the shades mix in this jubilant spree,
For hues filled with longing bring joy, don't you see?
In every soft corner, our laughter still rings,
In bursts of bright colors where nostalgia sings.

Faded photographs

In an album stacked with jests,
Old smiles peek from yellowed quests.
A cat in shorts, a duck in shoes,
Memories play like silly blues.

Frames with laughter, frames with grief,
Peeking noses, too much belief.
Snap a pic, and watch it fade,
Capture giggles that life made.

Who put the rim on that old hat?
Was it Uncle Joe or silly cat?
Snapshots shuffle through time's parade,
A gallery of the wild charade.

So here's to moments all askew,
With every laugh, old pain seems few.
Let the giggles from past times tease,
As we embrace our weird unease.

Remnants of Yesterday

Beneath the couch, where crumbs reside,
Rest the relics of fun we hide.
A sock that danced, a shoe that pranced,
Yesterday's laughter, too wild to chance.

The tipsy vase that lost its fight,
Flashed memories of a frantic night.
A story told with a wink and nudge,
Where even silence felt the grudge.

A half-eaten cake, an upside-down hat,
Echoes of chaos where we all sat.
Throwback moments, sprinkles and cheers,
The tales we weave dissolve our fears.

So let's revisit those silly days,
With bits of laughter in goofy ways,
Every crack and creak brings delight,
As remnants of joy take flight.

Hallowed Echoes

In the halls where laughter thrived,
Phantom giggles keep us alive.
Whispers of pranks and playful glares,
Hallowed echoes of joyful snares.

Worn-out shoes from the dance we shared,
Kites that flew when no one dared.
Their silent chatter, a punchline grand,
The stories linger, hand in hand.

Ticklish jests and silly fights,
Like shadows skipping through the nights.
They wiggle and twist 'til laughter bursts,
In hallowed halls where joy rehearsed.

Here's to the echoes we once drew,
To every grin that feels brand new.
We dance with ghosts of whimsy's spell,
In playful halls where memories dwell.

The Threads We Leave

We spin our tales with tangled yarns,
A ball of laughter, a heap of charms.
With every stitch, a story spins,
The fabric of chaos where humor wins.

Each knot we tie, a giggle sighed,
In threads of joy, our spirits ride.
A sweater made from mismatched days,
Together weaving our clumsy ways.

The quilt of mischief wraps us round,
In every patch, an echo found.
Count the stitches, silly or wise,
As life unravels before our eyes.

So gather 'round the colorful weave,
Celebrate the whimsy we believe.
With every thread, our legends grow,
A tapestry of the laughs we know.

Weaving Through Grief

In a world where giggles bloom,
I tripped on life's big silver spoon.
Laughter dances, masks in play,
As smiles get lost along the way.

Happiness wears socks that don't match,
While tears are caught in a silly batch.
The clown shoes squeak on every step,
Echoing laughter, a joyful prep.

We stitch our whims with threads so bright,
A patchwork heart, a comical sight.
Though shadows linger, we won't despair,
For chuckles nudge the heavy air.

In the dance of jests and slight distress,
We whirl around in a funny mess.
Each twist, a giggle, each turn, a roar,
Life's a circus, we're wanting more!

Boundless Emotions

Bubbles pop in the air so sweet,
While I chase giggles on silly feet.
Joy leaps higher than treetops tall,
As we skip around, having a ball.

An umbrella flips in a sudden gust,
And I tumble down—falling's a must.
Paint spills out in a rainbow flash,
Launching our dreams in quite the splash.

With hiccups bursting, we'll never pout,
Dealing with life in a funny scout.
Each punchline grows, amusing the crew,
A tapestry woven in vibrant hue.

Here's to our hearts in a wild embrace,
Where funny antics make joy take place.
With a wink and a wiggle, we'll stroll along,
Crafting our laughter, a garish song!

Whispered Goodbyes

A wave from the cat with a sassy tail,
Unruly goodbyes, they always prevail.
With bubblegum stuck on our shoes,
We giggle at life as it gets a bruise.

Slippers on the wrong feet, oh what a sight,
I waddle away, pretend it's all right.
With balloon animals lost in the breeze,
We cherish the moments, like slapstick tease.

A wink at the moon as we fumble through,
Kisses in whispers and laughter anew.
What's fleeting today may tomorrow bring,
In each silly tear, there's joy we can sing.

So let's toast to this clumsy disguise,
With hearts intertwined and ridiculous sighs.
Every sweet sorrow, a giggle in tow,
What life truly is, we'll always bestow!

Lament of the Unheld

Empty arms in a raucous dance,
While socks are mismatched, there's askance.
Fumbled hugs in a slapstick way,
With laughter caught where shadows play.

The bucket of smiles tipped upside down,
In a chaotic jive with a toddler clown.
Where pillows become beasts, all askew,
We wrestle our sorrows over a shoe.

With each giggle that escapes the core,
We paint the walls with painted "more."
Grinding our gears on the floor's slick run,
We chase after moments, laughter our gun.

So when the world feels a little too tight,
We'll tickle it's edges, ignite the light.
For in the mayhem where we might plead,
Laughter's our compass, it's all we need!

Between Hope and Heartbreak

I bought a ticket for the show,
But tripped on my own toe.
Hope danced just out of reach,
As my heart learned to screech.

I texted 'I'm on my way'
And got lost yesterday.
With hiccups and a grin,
I tried to fit right in.

Laughter filled the crowded room,
But my heart went boom, boom, boom.
A juggling act went wrong,
Turns out I don't belong.

Yet when the curtains close,
I laugh despite my woes.
For in this game of chance,
It's the stumble that leads to dance.

The Threads Unseen.

We weave our fates like crazy yarn,
Knots galore, a twisted charm.
A stitch here, a stitch there,
Oh look, my sock's a pair!

Each fray tells a funny tale,
Of times my plans set sail.
The needle's point, quite bold,
Yet somehow, I'm left cold.

Let's thread this needle without fear,
Wearing mismatched shoes, I cheer.
For in this cloth we share,
Life's fabric goes beyond compare.

And when the seams begin to show,
I laugh at life's grand show.
A tapestry of goofy glee,
Stitched in the quirks of 'me'.

Whispers in the Wind

The breeze said, 'Have a snack!'
As I tried to jog my track.
Chasing dreams while guzzling fries,
Wind tickles, and surprise!

With every gust, I tumble twice,
A dance of chaos, oh so nice.
The whispers tease my inner cheer,
As ketchup stains my shirt, oh dear!

A squirrel raced on by my side,
Challenging my silly stride.
I laughed as I lost the race,
With crumbs spread on my face.

Though winds may blow with playful guile,
I'll take each fall with a grin and style.
Let laughter be my lightest kin,
In breezy battles, I always win.

Frayed Connections

My Wi-Fi dropped, what a sad plight,
I waved goodbye to friends in sight.
Buffered hopes all went to waste,
While my snacks went to fast-paced haste.

Signal strength like a sad old cat,
Always lurking, imagine that!
I tried to connect with random flair,
But all I got was empty air.

The mouse danced like it had a spark,
While I fumbled in the dark.
My texts turned blurry, like a dream,
With a laugh, I tried to scream.

Yet here I sit, in this internet mess,
A true connoisseur of digital stress.
With ounce of giggles in my stock,
I'll keep on laughing around the clock.

www.ingramcontent.com/pod-product-compliance
Lightning Source LLC
Chambersburg PA
CBHW060123230426
43661CB00003B/312